# THE LIBRARY OF
# nutrition™

# Nutrition Sense
## Counting Calories, Figuring Out Fats, and Eating Balanced Meals

Linda Bickerstaff

rosen central

The Rosen Publishing Group, Inc., New York

*This book is dedicated to Margaret Flynn, Ph.D., nutritionist extraordinaire, University of Missouri School of Medicine, Columbia, MO.*

Published in 2005 by The Rosen Publishing Group, Inc.
29 East 21st Street, New York, NY 10010

### Library of Congress Cataloging-in-Publication Data
Bickerstaff, Linda.
Nutrition sense: counting calories, figuring out fats, and eating balanced meals / by Linda Bickerstaff. — 1st ed.
    p. cm. — (The Library of nutrition)
Includes bibliographical references.
ISBN 1-4042-0299-4 (library binding)
1. Food—Caloric content—Juvenile literature. 2. Food—Fat content—Juvenile literature.
I. Title. II. Series.
TX551.B48 2004
613.2—dc22
                                                                        2004014861

*Manufactured in the United States of America*

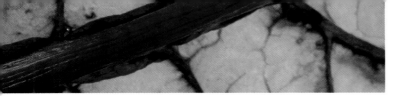

# contents

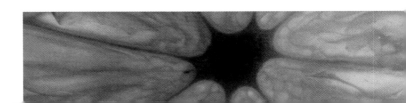

# introduction

Nutrition is the process of nourishing, by which organisms obtain energy (in the form of food) for growth, maintenance, and repair. It also refers to the study of food and diets. Good nutrition is the key to having the energy you need to do the things you want to do. In conjunction with exercise, it is essential to achieving your ideal body image. More important, proper nutrition is the foundation of good health.

One of every four American children is overweight; about half of those are considered obese. Obese children have many health problems, which are likely to continue into adulthood. The more you know about eating balanced meals, counting calories, and figuring out fats, the more control you will have over your own health and appearance today and in the future.

## Calories = Energy

Energy is everywhere. It is even stored in the foods we eat. The potential energy of food is converted or metabolized in our bodies into active or kinetic energy, measured as calories. This energy powers our brains, allows us to move, and helps us grow.

One calorie is the amount of heat needed to raise the temperature of a gram of water by one degree Celsius. When "calorie" is used in reference to diet or metabolic processes in our bodies, however, it means the large calorie or kilocalorie (kcal). A kilocalorie, sometimes designated by the use of a capital C, is the amount of heat needed to raise the temperature of a kilogram of water by one degree Celsius. When McDonald's says a Big Mac and medium fries contain 950 calories, this really refers to the number of kilocalories the meal has.

## Energy and Fats

Fats, or lipids, have gotten a bad rap. They are blamed for everything from bulging bathing suits to life-threatening heart attacks. However, fat can be used as energy by the body when glycogen (stored glucose) is depleted, or in the absence of carbohydrates. We can't live without fat in our diets. But because fat supplies twice as many calories as do protein and carbohydrates, eating too much fat packs on the pounds. Some types of fats are especially harmful to health and should be used sparingly.

## Balanced Meals

Well-balanced meals are those that supply the right amount of calories from a variety of foods. They are the key to proper nutrition, weight control, and optimal health. As you read this book, look for the answers to important questions such as: What nutrients and how many calories are found in different kinds of food? How do you know how many calories best meet your energy needs? Should you count calories? If so, how do you do this? Are there really "good" fats and "bad" fats? Can you eat a balanced meal, watch your calories and fats, and still have fun? How can you control your weight?

# chapter 1

# Food: Source of Nutrients and Calories

Foods contain chemical compounds called nutrients. Our bodies use nutrients to repair and grow body tissues. Nutrients also supply the calories needed for the hundreds of chemical processes that keep our bodies functioning.

## Nutrition: The Science of Food

Food scientists and research dieticians spend their working lives studying how our bodies use food and how food affects health. They have learned that the human diet contains as many as 100,000 chemical substances. Of these, only 300 are nutrients. Forty-nine of the nutrients are "essential nutrients" because they cannot be made by our bodies—they must be obtained from food. Essential nutrients include vitamins, minerals, some amino acids and fatty acids, and carbohydrates. Nonessential nutrients can be generated by the body from other compounds if we don't get enough of them in our diets.

The bulk of our diets consists of macronutrients, including proteins, carbohydrates, fats, water, and some minerals. Macronutrients are needed in relatively large quantities to build and repair tissues and provide energy. We also need small amounts of micronutrients for good health. These include vitamins and trace minerals.

## Proteins and Body Tissues

Proteins are complex organic compounds made from sequenced amino acids. They make up most of the tissues in the body. Amino acids contain carbon, hydrogen, oxygen, and nitrogen. Of the twenty amino acids in proteins, nine are essential amino acids, which must be obtained from food.

The amount of protein one needs varies with age. The recommended dietary allowance (RDA) for boys eleven to fourteen years old is 45 grams of protein daily; girls of the same age need 46 grams. This assumes that the protein is obtained from both animal and plant sources. Proteins from legumes (beans), grains (wheat, rice, corn), and root plants have fewer essential

Animal sources of protein such as meat, milk, and eggs are complete proteins because they contain all the essential amino acids. Plant sources of protein don't contain all the essential amino acids. However, you may get all the essential amino acids by eating a variety of plant-based foods.

---

**THE FOOD AND NUTRITION BOARD**

The Food and Nutrition Board makes recommendations about the amount of essential nutrients we need daily. It continuously reviews new scientific literature about essential nutrients and how they affect our health. Every five years, the Food and Nutrition Board issues revised RDAs to help people make healthy choices.

---

amino acids than those from meat, milk, and eggs. Vegetarians who don't eat any animal products must consume a lot more than 45 grams of protein each day to get an adequate amount of essential amino acids.

Proteins help repair and grow tissues while also supplying the body with energy. A gram of protein, regardless of its source, provides 4 kcal of energy. If you eat 100 grams of protein (about half a chicken breast, one egg, a cup of yogurt, and a cup of milk), your body will have 400 kcal of energy to use.

## Carbohydrates and Energy

Carbohydrates are important sources of energy. They are obtained mainly from foods such as grains (bread), legumes (beans or peas), and potatoes and other starchy vegetables. A gram of carbohydrates provides 4 kcal of energy.

Complex carbohydrates (starches) are found in whole grains, vegetables, and legumes. They metabolize slowly in the body to produce glucose. Glucose is the only substance that can provide energy to most organs of the body, especially the brain. A diet high in complex carbohydrates is good because complex carbohydrates are gradually broken down over several hours to provide the glucose your body needs for energy.

In recent years, carbohydrates have come under attack as a major reason why Americans are overweight. However, complex carbohydrates such as bread, pasta, and potatoes are the body's preferred source of energy.

A group of students eats lunch before a row of vending machines loaded with junk food at a high school in Chicago, Illinois. Some school systems have begun to limit the sale of junk food and carbonated drinks in their cafeterias.

## The Yo-Yo Effect

Simple carbohydrates are found in refined foods, such as white flour or granulated sugar, as well as in fructose—the sugar found in fruits and honey. They also provide energy. Eating too many simple carbohydrates, however, may lead to major problems in the body. They cause a rapid rise in blood-sugar levels, which stimulates special cells in the pancreas to secrete large amounts of insulin. Insulin is needed to enable the body to use glucose effectively. When too much insulin is secreted, it causes a rapid fall in blood glucose levels. This can result in the loss of pep and energy or even faintness. If you eat a candy bar to give yourself more pep, your blood sugar again skyrockets, your pancreas kicks out more insulin, your blood sugar falls, and, after a short while, you crash again. This yo-yo effect is very common in kids today because of the amount of simple carbohydrates they consume in junk food and soft drinks.

## Fat Is Needed for Good Health

Fats are very important to our diet. They are necessary for the production of many hormones in our bodies and to absorb fat-soluble vitamins and build nerve tissue. Fats provide more energy than any other type of food. Each gram of fat provides 9 kcal of energy. Stored fat in our bodies can be metabolized to provide energy when food is scarce or when our caloric requirements exceed our caloric intake—such as during strenuous exercise.

Fried foods, especially those served at fast-food restaurants, are full of fat—usually the dangerous kind. Nutritionists recommend that people should generally avoid fried foods. However, for the occasional treat, they suggest foods fried with peanut or olive oil.

Because fats contain twice as many calories per gram as carbohydrates or proteins, diets high in fat may lead to weight problems. Today, Americans get about 35 percent of their daily calories from fat. Most nutritionists believe this is too much. Kids are not exempt from this fat frenzy. Junk food is loaded with it.

# chapter 2

# Keeping an Eye on Calories

Counting calories is a lot of work. It is something that every overweight person must do to lose those extra pounds. To keep a healthy weight, you need to understand your daily calorie requirements and how various activities affect your energy needs. Then you can watch the calories you eat by checking food labels for calorie content, controlling portion sizes, and avoiding cooking methods that add calories.

You don't need to eat weird combinations of foods or special supplements to maintain your ideal weight and stay healthy. You just need to consume the same number of calories that you use. If you eat more calories than you burn, you will gain weight. If you eat too few, you will not only lose weight, but possibly muscle mass, energy, and, in extreme cases, life itself.

## How Many Calories Do You Need?

The number of calories each person needs is unique. No two people, including identical twins, are exactly alike. To

Reading food labels is an important part of counting calories. In addition to giving the amount of calories per serving, labels list the ingredients and give the percentage of the daily requirements of various nutrients.

determine how many calories you need, consider the following: your resting energy expenditure (REE), your activity level, your age, and, to some extent, your inherited body type.

In *The Teen Health Book*, Dr. Ralph Lopez writes, "Just as a parked car with an idling motor uses gas, so, too, does a body at rest consume calories." He notes that all of the metabolic processes our bodies constantly perform require energy. The number of calories our bodies require to do all these tasks is called resting energy expenditure. In general, eleven- to fourteen-year-olds must eat between 2,200 and 2,500 calories each day to provide the energy their bodies need to function. Older teen boys may need up to 3,000 calories to provide their bodies with fuel for basic functions.

## HOLLIDAY-SEGAR FORMULA USED TO ESTIMATE REE

The Holliday-Segar formula can be used to estimate REE, or caloric expenditures under resting or basal conditions.

The formula uses weight in kilograms. One kilogram equals 2.2 pounds.

For children weighing 10 kg or less,
> **REE = weight in kg x 100 calories**

For children weighing 11–20 kg,
> **REE = 1,000 cal + 50 cal per kg for each kg over 10**

For children weighing more than 20 kg,
> **REE = 1,500 cal + 20 cal per kg for each kg over 20**

For example, if you weigh 88 pounds (88 lb=40 kg), your REE would be 1,900 calories.
> **1,500 calories +**
> **400 calories (20 calories/kg x 20 kg) = 1,900 calories**

Once you have calculated your REE, figure out how many calories you burn during the day. By adding these to the REE, you will know the total number of calories you need daily. Dr. Lopez says that boys, eleven to fourteen, who are "normally active" need about 1,000 calories over their REE. Girls in the same age group need about 900 calories to provide energy for normal activities. If you exercise vigorously or are involved in sports, you will need additional calories. However, inactive youths need far fewer calories. In general, active eleven- to fourteen-year-old boys need 2,500 to 3,000 calories daily. Girls in that age group need about 2,200 calories daily.

Soccer star Mia Hamm kicks a soccer ball at a playground in Washington, D.C., during the launch of the privately sponsored Get Kids in Action initiative to prevent childhood obesity. Exercise and proper nutrition are essential to good health.

## Keeping an Eye on Calorie Intake

Reading food labels will help you keep track of the number of calories you eat. By law, food labels must list the number of calories per serving as well as the number of servings in the can or package. However, food label information is not standardized. Therefore, it is important to note what the serving size is.

Almost every book on nutrition contains lists of food and the calorie content of each. These compilations are also available on numerous Web sites and can be obtained from government publications. However, there is an easier way to keep an eye on calories. If you lump foods into food groups and know how many calories are in foods of a particular group, you have a lot less to remember.

Most nutritionists place foods into one of six categories: 1) carbohydrates from bread, cereal, rice, and pasta; 2) fruits; 3) vegetables; 4) dairy products; 5) proteins from meat, poultry, fish, beans, eggs, and nuts; and 6) fats, oils, and sweets. Each category is assigned a single calorie value per serving. For instance, a serving of vegetables has 25 calories, while a serving of fruit has 60 calories. Dairy products and proteins are assigned 110 calories per serving. Carbohydrates have 80 calories per serving. Fats, oils, and sweets are assigned 45 calories per serving. Knowing how many servings you consume daily in each food group makes it easy to estimate the number of calories. With a little practice, you will become an expert on calculating serving sizes and caloric intake.

If you eat a half-cup of cooked cereal with a sliced banana and a cup of low-fat milk for breakfast, you have consumed 240 calories (cereal = 80 calories, banana = 60 calories, milk = 110 calories). By becoming aware of the general calorie content of foods and developing

# What Constitutes a Serving?

The National Institutes of Health (NIH) gives the following serving sizes in the various food categories:

### Bread, Cereal, Rice, and Pasta Group

1 slice bread
1 cup ready-to-eat cereal
1/2 cup cooked cereal, rice, or pasta

### Milk, Yogurt, and Cheese Group

1 cup low-fat milk or yogurt
1 1/2 ounces natural cheese
2 ounces processed cheese

### Vegetable Group

1 cup raw vegetables or
1/2 cup frozen leafy vegetables (cooked)
1/2 cup other vegetables (cooked or raw)
3/4 cup vegetable juice

### Fruit Group

1 medium apple, banana, or orange
1/2 cup chopped, cooked, or canned fruit
3/4 cup fruit juice

### Meat, Poultry, Fish, Dry Beans, and Nuts

2–3 oz. cooked lean meat, poultry, or fish
1/2 cup cooked dry beans
1 egg
2 tablespoons peanut butter
1/3 cup nuts

The NIH recommends that you use fats, oils, and sweets sparingly.

Most people who eat at fast-food restaurants have no idea how many calories they consume with each meal. The larger fast-food chains post the calorie content of their most popular meals on their Web sites.

good eating habits early, good nutrition and normal weight will be yours for life.

When you eat a well-balanced meal at home, it is relatively easy to keep track of calories. Counting calories when you eat out is more difficult. Eating at a fine restaurant or even a fast-food joint or pizza parlor on occasion is a treat that should not be denied. But making a daily habit of eating fast food or overeating at fine restaurants is a sure way of gaining unwanted weight.

# chapter 3

# Figuring Out Fats

E veryone knows what fat is. It's that whitish yellow part of steak or what gets on your face and hands when you eat fried chicken. It's also the body tissue that creates those unwanted bulges around your waist and thighs. Chemically, fats are large molecules made up of varying numbers of fatty acids connected together.

In an online article entitled "How Fat Works," Marshall Brain explains, "A fatty acid is a long hydrocarbon chain capped by a carboxyl group." To understand this, imagine two apples sitting on a table connected by a toothpick at their centers. Sticking out of each apple are three other toothpicks. On the first apple, a marshmallow is attached to one of the three toothpicks and grapes are attached to the other two. Grapes are attached to all three toothpicks on the second apple. The apples represent the element carbon (C), the grapes represent hydrogen (H) ions, and the toothpicks represent the bonds that hold the parts together. This is a hydrocarbon unit. The marshmallow represents the carboxyl group. Such groups contain carbon, hydrogen, and oxygen, and they are indicated by the chemical formula, COOH. All organic acids contain a carboxyl group. The simple acid represented by our

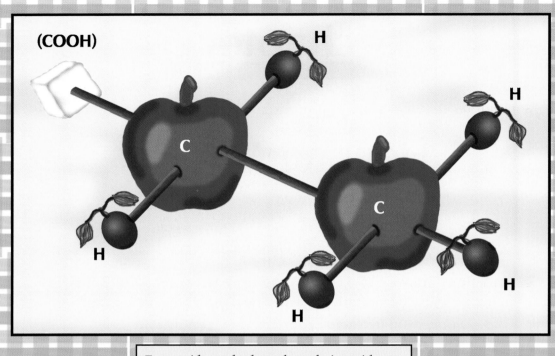

**(COOH)**

H

H

C

C

H

H

H

Fatty acids are hydrocarbon chains with an organic acid group (COOH) at the end

apple model, which has only two hydrocarbon units, is called propionic acid, which is often used as a preservative in food.

Fatty acids, the building blocks of fats, are also made of carbon, hydrogen, and a carboxyl group. If you constructed a model of stearic acid—a fatty acid that is one component of the fats in our diets—it would look just like our model of acetic acid except it would have seventeen apples (or carbons) connected together instead of just two.

There are many kinds of fat in the foods we eat. For instance, butter, margarine, lard, olive oil, and various cooking oils are all fats. These fats differ from each other by the types of fatty acids from which they are made. The difference does not end there, however. For example, at room temperature butter and lard are solids, margarine is a semisolid, and olive and other cooking oils are liquid. Whether a fat is solid, semisolid, or liquid at room temperature depends on the bonds (the toothpicks) that hold the hydrocarbons together. Solid fats (butter, lard) are saturated fats because all bonds are tightly attached to something (carbon, hydrogen, or carboxyl group). Saturated fats are known as "bad" fats. Liquid fats are unsaturated fats because some of their bonds are not tightly attached at both ends to a carbon, hydrogen, or carboxyl group. These bonds, under certain conditions, can become unattached at their loose connections leaving them free to attach to something other than a carbon, hydrogen, or carboxyl group. Unsaturated fats are known as "good" fats.

From left to right: two sticks of butter, a bottle of oil, and a scoop of shortening. As a general rule, the more solid the fat, the more hazardous it may be to your health.

## Fat: A Bone of Contention in the Scientific Community

Much controversy exists among nutritionists about how much and what kinds of fat should be eaten daily. Some scientists believe that saturated

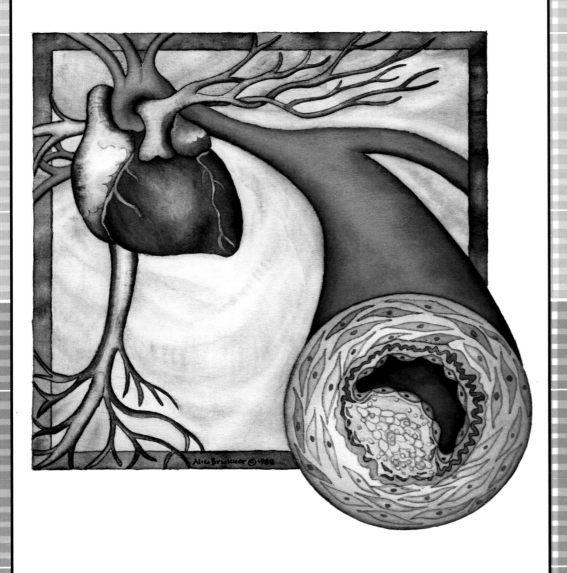

This illustration shows a cross-section of a clogged artery. Bad fats can clog arteries like grease in a kitchen sink drain. When this happens, the flow of blood is obstructed, increasing the risk of life-threatening illnesses and mental decline.

fat should be avoided completely. They believe that the large amount of saturated fat found in many Americans' diets is responsible, in large part, for the high number of heart attacks and strokes in the nation. These so-called bad fats clog the arteries that carry blood to the heart and brain, leading to heart attacks and strokes. Nutritionists recommend that unsaturated fats such as olive oil or canola oil—the "good" fats—be used for cooking rather than butter or lard, which are saturated fats.

Other scientists disagree. They believe that saturated fats are not as bad as some say. They note that people in other nations, such as France, eat more saturated fat than do Americans, yet the French have a lower incidence of heart attack and stroke deaths than Americans do.

Much research is being done to learn the truth. You will undoubtedly hear more about such studies. Not all of the information you read or hear will be true, so remember to evaluate the data carefully. In the meantime, your total intake of fat should account for less than 30 percent of the total number of calories you eat daily. Also, 10 percent or less of the calories should come from saturated fat.

## Fats Are Important

Nutritionists do agree on two things. The first is that people must have some fat in their diet to be healthy. In her book *The Complete Idiot's Guide to Total Nutrition*, Joy Bauer lists various reasons why "fat is fabulous."

> Fat provides you with a ready source of energy. Children need fat to grow properly. Fat supports the cell walls within our bodies. Fat enables your body to circulate, store, and absorb the fat-soluble vitamins A, D, E, and K. Without any fat, you would become deficient [in these vitamins]. Fat supplies essential fatty

acids that your body can't make and must therefore get from food. Fat helps promote healthy skin and hair. Fat makes food taste better by adding flavor, texture, and aroma. Fat provides a layer of insulation just beneath the skin. People who are extremely thin are often cold because they lack this layer of sub-cutaneous fat . . . Fat surrounds your vital organs for protection and support.

Fat is needed for other things within the body as well. One of the most important is the building of body tissue, especially in the nervous system. Fats are also critical in the manufacture of hormones. We cannot live without fat in our diets.

## Too Many Calories from Fat

The second area of agreement among most scientists is that Americans get too many calories from fat. Since fats provide twice as many calories as carbohydrates and proteins, diets that are high in fat are also high in calories. Most Americans now get more than 35 percent of their calories from fat. Even kids are eating a lot more fat now than they did in the past. Most fast foods contain large amounts of fat. Many schools have shortened lunch periods from an hour to a half hour. As a result, kids have to eat in a hurry. Some schools allow fast-food franchises to set up shop in or near their cafeterias. Hamburgers and fries with a soft drink can be obtained quickly for a fast lunch. Also, many kids prefer fast foods over other foods offered in cafeterias.

Nutritionists recommend limiting your fat intake to 30 percent of your total daily calories. For active eleven- to fourteen-year-olds, this amounts to 70 to 100 grams.

# chapter 4

# Eating Balanced Meals

E ating balanced meals and making wise food choices are critical. According to Dr. Kenneth Cooper, author of *Kid Fitness*, "The main idea here is to establish lifetime eating habits that are rooted in positive choices rather than promoting a restrictive dieting mentality."

Making the right food choices may sound like a tough thing to do. It can be difficult when you are surrounded by fast-food restaurants, snack foods loaded with calories and fat, and enough soda to float a battleship. Where do you start establishing healthy eating habits? A good place to start is to learn to eat balanced meals. What are they? Who decides what constitutes a balanced meal? Can eating still be fun? Here are some answers to help you begin to establish a lifetime of proper eating habits.

## USDA Dietary Guidelines

The U.S. Department of Agriculture (USDA) and the U.S. Department of Health and Human Services (HHS) have jointly developed a set of dietary guidelines for all Americans older than two years of age. These guidelines, based on current advice from nutritionists, form the basis for many federal nutrition policies. The guidelines include the following:

A balanced meal, made up of all the food groups, is usually a colorful meal.

○ Eat a variety of foods to get the energy, protein, vitamins, minerals, and fiber you need for good health.

○ Balance the food you eat with physical activity. Maintain or improve your weight to reduce your chances of having high blood pressure, heart disease, a stroke, certain cancers, and the most common forms of diabetes.

○ Choose a diet with plenty of grain products, vegetables, and fruits. These provide needed vitamins, minerals, fiber, and complex carbohydrates, and they can help you lower your intake of fat.

○ Choose a diet moderate in sugar. A diet with lots of sugars has too many calories and too few nutrients for most people and can contribute to tooth decay.

○ Choose a diet moderate in salt and sodium to help reduce your risk of high blood pressure.

## The Food Guide Pyramid

In 1992 the USDA developed the food guide pyramid to support these dietary guidelines. According to its developers,

> The pyramid is based on USDA's research on what foods Americans eat, what nutrients are in these foods and how to make the best food choices for you. The pyramid is an outline of what to eat each day. It's not a rigid prescription, but a general guide that lets you choose a healthful diet that's right for you. The pyramid calls for eating a variety of foods to get the nutrients you need and at the same time the right amount of calories to maintain or improve your weight. The pyramid also focuses on fat because most American diets are too high in fat, especially saturated fats.

Eating a balanced diet encourages you to consume a variety of foods. This is why the food guide pyramid is so helpful. When using it, you will find that all the food groups are equally important. You need foods from each group, but in differing amounts.

# The Food Pyramid

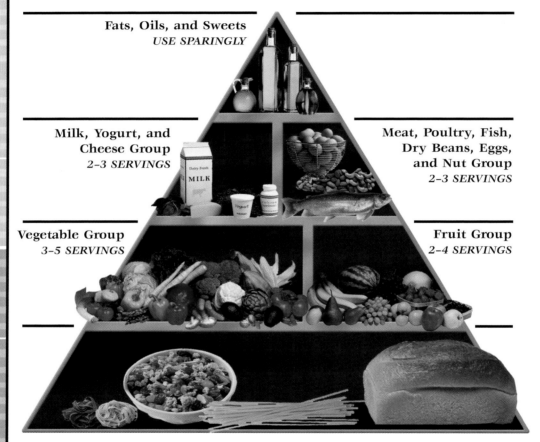

**Fats, Oils, and Sweets**
*USE SPARINGLY*

**Milk, Yogurt, and Cheese Group**
*2–3 SERVINGS*

**Meat, Poultry, Fish, Dry Beans, Eggs, and Nut Group**
*2–3 SERVINGS*

**Vegetable Group**
*3–5 SERVINGS*

**Fruit Group**
*2–4 SERVINGS*

**Bread, Cereal, Rice, and Pasta Group**
*6–11 SERVINGS*

Understanding the food pyramid can help you develop healthy eating habits. In response to criticism that the pyramid is too vague, the federal government is revising it to be more helpful to the general public.

## Complex Carbohydrates Make a Strong Base

At the base of the pyramid are the complex carbohydrates—bread, cereal, rice, and pasta. They appear at the bottom because they provide you with a good energy base on which to build a balanced diet. You should eat six to eleven servings of foods in this category daily. Complex carbohydrates are the best source of energy available. Think of complex carbohydrates as time-release energy capsules. By eating six to eleven of these "capsules" throughout the day, you will have energy to sustain your activities.

## Fruits and Vegetables

The fruit and vegetable groups make up the next level of the pyramid. Vegetables are important sources of vitamins and some of the needed micronutrients, such as iron and magnesium. Vegetables contain little or no fat. Particularly good sources of dietary fiber, vegetables keep the digestive system working properly.

The food pyramid recommends eating two to four servings of fruit daily. Fruits are great sources of vitamins A and C as well as a primary source of dietary potassium, which is needed for many chemical reactions in our bodies. Fruits are also low in fat and sodium.

## Protein-Rich Foods

The next level of the pyramid includes foods high in protein. Dairy group products are good sources of protein and calcium, which is necessary for proper bone growth. Although the food pyramid suggests two to three servings from this group daily, choosing products made with reduced-fat milk will decrease the amount of calories and fat you eat while obtaining the protein and calcium.

The various types of vegetables at this produce stand make for a colorful display. In addition to their nutritional values, vegetables make meals more appealing in color. When overcooked, however, they decline in taste, color, and nutritional value.

Meats, poultry, and fish are also excellent sources of protein. Many people who avoid meat eat legumes (dried beans and peas) as their primary source of dietary protein. Although legumes are vegetables, they are included in the meat, poultry, and fish group because of their high protein content. However, proteins from legumes are not as rich in essential amino acids as are meat proteins. Vegetarians must keep this in mind when planning their diets. Besides proteins, foods in this group provide many of the B vitamins as well as iron and zinc. The pyramid suggests two to three servings from this food category daily.

## Minimize Foods at the Peak of the Pyramid

At the peak of the pyramid are fats, oils, and sweets. The dietary guidelines recommend consuming items in this group sparingly. The USDA states that you will obtain half the fat you need even if you eat the lowest-fat choices from each food group on the pyramid and add no fat in food preparation or at the table.

Consider carefully how you want to get your remaining fat calories. The USDA, which recommends unsaturated rather than saturated fats, notes that saturated fats should be limited to 10 percent of your calories or one-third of your total fat intake.

## Breakfast

Eating a well-balanced meal is a step in the right direction, but not if you do it just once a day! You've probably heard people say: "Eat your breakfast! It's the most important meal of the day." They're right! Breakfast provides your body with energy after an eight- to ten-hour period of fasting. While you don't expend many exercise calories while you sleep, your body still uses a lot of energy for its metabolic functions.

Skipping breakfast is like forgetting to put gas in a car when the gauge reads "empty." Although you may not cease functioning, you may feel terrible and have very little pep. Breakfast is the time to eat those time-release energy capsules, complex carbohydrates.

Three meals a day are a tradition in America. Many nutritionists believe this is not the best way to eat. They note that three meals a day give people most of their energy in three bursts. Between these bursts people lack energy. To compensate for feeling tired, someone might eat a candy bar or some cookies between meals. This provides an energy boost but also increases one's calories and, over time, one's weight. These nutritionists suggest we become "grazers." Instead of eating three large meals daily, consume small amounts throughout the day. This may not be possible during the school year, but mid-morning and after-school snacks are not a bad idea. Make the energy from those snacks last by avoiding simple sugars and the yo-yo effect!

# chapter 5

# Obesity, a National Health Problem: How to Avoid It

O besity is defined as an excessive accumulation of body
fat. It can lead to physical problems. For instance,
obesity is the leading cause of high blood pressure in young
adults. It is also causing many kids to develop "adult onset"
or type II diabetes. Diabetes is a metabolic disease that con-
tributes to heart attacks, strokes, blindness, and kidney fail-
ure in relatively young adults. Fortunately, obesity can be
avoided or, if you are already overweight, corrected!

## Are You Overweight or Obese?

Dr. Ralph Lopez notes, "One way of defining our weight as
normal is to proportion it to our height." To do this, divide
your weight as measured in kilograms by your height as
measured in meters squared. This calculation is called
your body mass index (BMI).

Weight-loss camps have become more common throughout the United States in response to a growing concern about obesity, especially in children and teens. Participants learn how to achieve and maintain a healthy weight through proper exercise and nutrition.

The Centers for Disease Control and Prevention (CDC) publishes growth charts to compare BMIs in kids. Dr. Lopez suggests another way to evaluate your BMI. He says, "A rule of thumb is that your BMI should be between 22 and 23 in order to be average." He also observes that a BMI lower than 20 suggests you are underweight, while a BMI of 25 to 29 indicates you are overweight. If your BMI is between 30 and 35, you are obese. BMI, like any other calculation, should be used with common sense. A very muscular person, such as a wrestler, may have a BMI in the overweight range because muscle weighs more than fat.

> ## FOUR STEPS FOR CALCULATING BMI
>
> 1. Your weight in pounds divided by 2.2 = your weight in kilograms.
>    **example: 100 lbs / 2.2 = 45 kg**
>
> 2. Your height in inches x 0.0254 = your height in meters
>    **example: 60 inches x 0.0254 = 1.524 m**
>
> 3. Multiply height in meters by itself to get meters squared.
>    **example: 1.524 m x 1.524 m = 2.323 m$^2$**
>
> 4. Divide #1 by # 3 to get your BMI.
>    **example: 45/2.323 =19.37**

## How Big of a Problem Is Obesity?

In the article "Evaluation and Treatment of Childhood Obesity," Dr. Rebecca Moran reports on the findings of several health surveys, including the National Health and Nutrition Examination Surveys. She explains: "The prevalence of childhood obesity is estimated to be 25–30 percent. Furthermore, over the years encompassed by these surveys, the prevalence of obesity has increased by 54 percent in children six to eleven years of age and by 39 percent in adolescents 12–17 years of age." Teenagers who are overweight have a 70 percent chance of being overweight or obese as adults.

Obesity is reaching epidemic proportions among kids and adults in the United States. This is of great concern. But, by controlling your weight and establishing good eating habits now, you will be much healthier as an adult. Most kids have long-range goals for college, careers, and families of their own. Why not have health goals to avoid diabetes, heart disease, strokes, and the many types of cancer associated with obesity?

Regardless of your size, it is important to be aware of your weight and how it fluctuates. Gaining or losing weight too quickly can be hazardous to your health.

# What Causes Obesity?

The cause of obesity is simple. If you consistently eat more calories than you burn, you gain weight. Dr. Moran explains: "By measure, 3,500 calories is equivalent to one pound [of body weight]; thus, an excess intake of only 50 to 100 calories per day will lead to a five to ten pound weight gain over one year. As a result, a relatively small imbalance between energy input and output can lead to significant weight gain over time. In fact, most obese children demonstrate a slow but consistent weight gain over several years." She also says, "The best way to significantly affect the prevalence of obesity is to prevent it."

# Preventing Obesity

Here are five suggestions to help you maintain a normal body weight. If you have checked your BMI and you already fall into the overweight or obese categories, these suggestions will help you lose weight over time.

**1. Don't be a junk food junkie.** Kids today may not be eating any more than kids did in the past. In fact, in many cases, you eat less. It is what you eat that creates the problem. A lunch packed at home consisting of carrot sticks, a ham sandwich on whole wheat bread, an apple, and money for a carton of 2 percent milk isn't as exciting as a fast-food hamburger, medium order of fries, and a twelve-ounce cola offered at the school cafeteria. Most kids go for the burger without a second thought.

Comparing the calorie content of the two lunches is eye-opening. The home-packed lunch totals 455 calories and approximately 10 grams of fat. In the article "Fast Food Pitfalls," Bruce Mirken says that the

It may be difficult to avoid junk food when everyone around you eats it. It may help to have an eating partner who shares the same healthful goals that you have.

burger and fries contain 1,040 calories while the cola adds 150 for a total of 1,190 calories and 59 grams of fat. So, one big fast-food burger meal contains more than half of the RDA of calories for kids your age and about 83 percent of your RDA for fat. If you stay within your RDA for calories (2,200 to 2,800), you can't eat much else the rest of the day!

**2. Stay active.** Dance a lot. Or if dancing is out, ride a bike, take a hike, or fly a kite! Did you know that you burn as many as 300 calories an hour dancing? Walking, roller-skating, swimming, and even bowling for an hour expend nearly the same number of calories. More vigorous activities like skiing, tennis, handball, or bicycling burn even more calories.

Try to avoid eating while watching the television or using the computer.

Runners expend a whopping 900 calories an hour. The bottom line is to start moving! Make exercise a regular part of your daily activities. Not only does exercise expend calories, but it also releases endorphins, which pump you up and brighten your day.

**3. Don't make food the center of your life.** Many people eat just to be eating. It is something to do when we are bored. Eating is also a sociable activity. How often do you plan to meet friends for lunch or at a pizza joint after school? While this is one way to keep in touch with your friends, it can lead to calorie overload. It's hard to resist food when it smells good and everyone else is eating. Meet your friends at the skateboard center or at the park where you can hang out without food being the center attraction.

**4. Turn off the television and computer.** Getting away from the television or computer screen gives you time to pursue more active interests and decreases the amount of time that you are being manip-

It is important to make exercise a part of your daily routine. Working out with friends rather than alone tends to make it easier and more fun.

ulated by advertisers. Media advertisers are geniuses at persuading us to do things and buy things, including high-calorie foods, we neither want nor need.

**5. Take the time to learn about nutrition and health.** Getting serious about eating the right stuff is the best gift you can possibly give yourself. Read food labels in the grocery store. Check out the Web sites of fast-food franchises to see what is really in the food you love to eat. Think about people you know who have diabetes or heart disease or who have had strokes. Determine to avoid these problems in your life. Be the advocate for healthy eating in your family and among your friends. Take control of your life!

# Glossary

**advocate** To plead in favor of; to support.

**carbon** A nonmetallic chemical element that occurs in all organic matter.

**deficient** Lacking in some quality necessary for completeness.

**endorphin** Any of several substances secreted in the brain that have pain-relieving qualities like those of the drug morphine.

**expenditure** That which is used up or consumed.

**grazer** One who eats small amounts frequently throughout the day.

**guidelines** A set of rules or suggestions to direct a course of action.

**hormone** A chemical substance produced in one part of the body which, when transported through the bloodstream, has a specific effect on the activity of a certain organ.

**junkie** A slang term referring to an addict.

**legume** Any of a large group of plants in the pea family.

**metabolic** Related to the chemical changes in living cells, by which energy is provided for the vital processes and activities of the cells.

**minerals** Any of a number of nonorganic substances that are needed in small quantities for proper metabolism.

**pitfall**  A danger, difficulty, or error into which one may fall unsuspectingly.

**prevalence**  How frequently something occurs or how widespread it is.

**standardize**  To compare with or conform to a set of rules or criteria.

**supplements**  Foods or other nutritious elements added to a diet to fill deficiencies in that diet.

**vitamins**  Any of a number of naturally occurring constituents of food that are needed in small quantities for proper metabolism.

# For More Information

**American Academy of Pediatrics**
141 Northwest Point Boulevard
Elk Grove Village, IL 60007
(847) 434-4000
Web site: http://www.aap.org

**Center for Science in the Public Interest**
**Nutrition Action Health Letter**
1875 Connecticut Avenue NW, Suite 300
Washington, DC 20009
Web site: http://cspinet.org/nah

**Food and Nutrition Information Center**
U.S. Department of Agriculture
National Agriculture Library, Room 105
10301 Baltimore Avenue
Beltsville, MD 20705
(301) 504-5719
Web site: http://www.nal.usda.gov/fnic

**National Center for Nutrition and Dietetics**
**American Dietetic Association**
216 West Jackson Boulevard
Chicago, IL 60606-6995

Consumer Nutrition Hotline: (800) 366-1655
Web site: http://www.eatright.org/Public

**The President's Council on Physical Fitness and Sports**
Department W
200 Independence Avenue SW
Washington, DC 20201
(202) 690-9000
Web site: http://www.fitness.gov

**Weight Control Information Network**
1 Win Way
Bethesda, MD 20892-3665
(202) 828-1025
E-mail: win@info.niddk.nih.gov
Web site: http://www.niddk.nih.gov/health/nutrit/winbro/winbro1.html

**Web Sites**
Due to the changing nature of Internet links, the Rosen Publishing Group, Inc., has developed an online list of Web sites related to the subject of this book. This site is updated regularly. Please use this link to access the list:

http://www.rosenlinks.com/linu/nuse

# For Further Reading

Bauer, Joy. *The Complete Idiot's Guide to Total Nutrition.* New York: Alpha Books, 1999.

Cooper, Kenneth H. *Kid Fitness: A Complete Shape-up Program from Birth Through High School.* New York: Bantam Books, 1991.

Henner, Marilu, with Lorin Henner. *Healthy Kids: Help Them Eat Smart and Stay Active—For Life!* New York: Regan Books, 2001.

Jacobson, Michael E., and Jayne G. Hurley. *Restaurant Confidential: The Shocking Truth About What You're Really Eating When You're Eating Out.* New York: Workman Publishing, 2002.

Lopez, Ralph I. *The Teen Health Book: A Parents' Guide to Adolescent Health and Well-Being.* New York: W. W. Norton and Company, 2002.

Schwager, Tina, and Michele Schuerger. *The Right Moves: A Girl's Guide to Getting Fit and Feeling Good.* Minneapolis: Free Spirit Publishing, 1998.

Seixas, Judith S. *Junk Food—What It Is, What It Does.* New York: Greenwillow Books, 1984.

# Bibliography

Bauer, Joy. *The Complete Idiot's Guide to Total Nutrition.* New York: Alpha Books, 1999.

"BMI for Children and Teens." Centers for Disease Control and Prevention. Retrieved November 2003 (http://www.cdc.gov/nccdphp/dnpa/bmi/bmi-for-age.htm).

Brain, Marshall. *How Fat Works.* Howstuffworks.com. Retrieved November 2003 (http://health.howstuffworks.com/fat/htm).

Cooper, Kenneth H. *Kid Fitness: A Complete Shape-up Program from Birth Through High School.* New York: Bantam Books, 1991.

Freudenrich, Craig. *How Fat Cells Work.* Howstuffworks.com. Retrieved November 2003 (http://health.howstuffworks.com/fat-cell.htm).

Henner, Marilu, with Lorin Henner. *Healthy Kids: Help Them Eat Smart and Stay Active—For Life!* New York: Regan Books, 2001.

Lopez, Ralph I. *The Teen Health Book: A Parents' Guide to Adolescent Health and Well-Being.* New York: W. W. Norton and Company, 2002.

Medical Food News. "Saturated Fats, Monounsaturated Fats and Polyunsaturated Fats." Retrieved November 2003 (http://www.medicinalfoodnews.com/vol01/issue7/sat_fat.htm).

Mirken, Bruce. *Fast Food Pitfalls.* BluePrint for Health. Retrieved November 2003 (http://blueprint.bluecrossmn.com/topic/fastfoodpitfalls).

Moran, Rebecca. *Evaluation and Treatment of Childhood Obesity.* American Family Physician. Retrieved November 2003 (http://www.aafp.org/afp/990215ap/861.html).

Schwager, Tina, and Michele Schuerger. *The Right Moves: A Girl's Guide to Getting Fit and Feeling Good.* Minneapolis: Free Spirit Publishing, 1998.

Woolston, Chris. *School Lunches: Invasion of the Body Fatteners.* BluePrint for Health. Retrieved November 2003 (http://blueprint.bluecrossmn.com/topic/schoollunch).

# Index

## About the Author

Linda Bickerstaff, M.D., a retired surgeon, writes from her home in Ponca City, Oklahoma.

## Photo Credits

Cover (background images), back cover images, pp. 1 (background images), 3, 4, 12, 19, 25, 32, 40, 42, 44, 45, 47 © David Wasserman/Artville; cover image, p. 1 © LWA/ Stephen Welstead/Corbis; pp. 7, 17, 28 © Photodisc/2004 Punchstock; p. 9 © James Noble/Getty Images; pp. 10, 15, 33, 37 © Getty Images News/Getty Images; p. 11 © William Taufic/Corbis; pp. 13, 26, 38 © Photodisc Green/Getty Images; p. 18 © Ariel Skelley/Corbis; p. 20 Geri Fletcher; p. 21 © 2004 Punchstock; p. 22 © Royalty-Free Corbis; p. 28 © Photodisc/2004 Punchstock except image of fish © Image Club; p. 30 © Wolfgang Kaehler/Corbis; p. 35 © Steve Prezant/Corbis; p. 39 © Tom Stewart/Corbis.

**Designer:** Geri Fletcher; **Editor:** Wayne Anderson